Angels

Tone Finnanger

D&C
David and Charles

A DAVID & CHARLES BOOK

Copyright © J.W. Cappelens Forlag, AS 2010
Cappelen Hobby
www.cappelen.no

First published in the UK in 2010 by David & Charles
Reprinted in 2011, 2013, 2014, 2016, 2017, 2018

David & Charles is an imprint of F&W Media International, Ltd
Pynes Hill Court, Pynes Hill, Exeter, EX2 5AZ

F&W Media International, Ltd is a subsidiary of F+W Media, Inc
10151 Carver Road, Suite #200, Blue Ash, OH 45242, USA

Content and images first published in *Crafting Tilda's Friends*, *Sew Sunny Homestyle*, *Sew Pretty Homestyle*, *Sew Pretty Christmas Homestyle*, *Crafting Springtime Gifts* and *Crafting Christmas Gifts*.

A catalogue record for this book is available from the British Library.

ISBN-13: 978-0-7153-3874-2 hardback
ISBN-10: 0-7153-3874-9 hardback

Printed in China by RR Donnelley
for F&W Media International, Ltd
Pynes Hill Court, Pynes Hill, Exeter, EX2 5AZ

Publisher Ali Myer
Acquisitions Editor Jennifer Fox-Proverbs
Assistant Editor Jeni Hennah
Project Editor Beth Dymond
Design Manager Sarah Clark
Production Controller Bev Richardson
Pre Press Jodie Culpin

F+W Media publish high quality books on a wide range of subjects.
For more great book ideas visit: **www.sewandso.co.uk**

www.ilovetilda.com
For beauty and inspiration in everything Tilda

CONTENTS

Fabrics and Materials

Fabrics

Fabrics with a slightly coarse weave are better for making stuffed figures than thin or fine fabrics, as they are much firmer and therefore easier to mould. Linen and plain cotton fabrics are the best types to use, and fabrics with a woven pattern are often preferable to printed patterns. If you would like to use thinner fabrics, you may find it useful to iron a layer of fusible interfacing on the wrong side, to give you a firmer fabric.

When choosing material for the skin colour, use pale linen to create a fair skin tone and light brown linen for darker skin tones. If you are making animals, try using a material with stripes or spots to create an interesting fur effect.

The designs that do not require stuffing, as well as the clothes for the figures and the appliqué projects, can be made from cottons, polyester cottons and most types of fabric. These can therefore be much more decorative than the fabrics used for the stuffed figures.

Fabrics can be bought from craft shops, patchwork and quilting suppliers, and even some department stores. You could also try shops that sell fabrics for curtains and upholstery, which are often a good source for classic patterns and French Toile.

Stuffing

For the projects in this book you will need a good-quality polyester stuffing to fill the figures. A selection of stuffing and wadding can be purchased from most patchwork and quilting shops, as well as from many online retailers.

Fusible interfacing

Fusible interfacing comes in various thicknesses to suit different projects. Volume interfacing is an iron-on fusible wadding (batting) that produces a firm, padded result. Lightweight interfacing is much thinner and is used for stiffening or reinforcing lighter fabrics. Firm interfacing is used for making fabric boxes and large bags, so that the items will stand upright without collapsing. For the best results, choose a fusible interfacing that is slightly lighter in weight than your fabric.

Iron-on adhesive

Bondaweb is a strong double-sided adhesive, which bonds one fabric to another when ironed. The adhesive side is pressed against the reverse side of a material and the paper is torn off, resulting in an adhesive material for simple appliqué work. You can also buy Wonderweb iron-on tape, which is useful for attaching smaller pieces of fabric, such as adding trims.

Accessories

A huge variety of beads, ribbons, buttons and other embellishments can be found in craft shops, or you can collect natural materials to decorate your projects. Tilda products, such as mini gold crowns and dolls' hair, are available from www.pandurohobby.co.uk.

Useful tools

- **A vanishing ink pen**
  Useful for tracing patterns onto fabric. The line disappears when you press it with a damp cloth or after a short while. Alternatively, you can use a fine waterproof fabric pen, or a white gel roller-ball pen for darker fabrics.

- **Small pointed fabric scissors**
  Vital for getting precise shapes when cutting out material.

- **A transparent sewing machine foot**
  Makes it easier to see and follow the pattern that has been traced onto the fabric.

- **A wooden plant stick**
  Useful for turning figures the right way out and inserting stuffing.

- **Craft paints**
  Used for creating faces for the figures and adding details to the clothes and accessories.

Templates

All templates at the back of this book need to be enlarged by 400%. Add seam allowance for all templates, unless otherwise stated.

For details of craft shops and suppliers, please refer to the list on page 46.

Stuffed Forms

Hair

Insert pins on top and down the back of the head, then insert one pin either side of the head. Twist the hair back and forth between the two pins on either side of the head, making sure that you cover the whole head, see Figure A. Stitch the hair to the head and remove the pins. Make a loop on either side of the head and stitch in place at the top and a little way down, see Figure B. Make two balls of hair and stitch to either side of the head, see Figure C.

Faces

It is always best to wait until the hair, ears and any headdresses are in place before you add the face. This makes it easier for you to see where the eyes should be positioned. Insert two pins in the head where the eyes should be. Remove the pins and fix the eyes in the pinholes, using the eye tool from a face kit or the head of a pin dipped in black paint. Blusher or lipstick can be applied with a dry brush to create rosy cheeks.

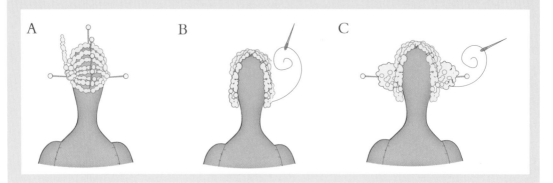

SEWING

Avoid cutting out the item first unless absolutely necessary. Fold the fabric double, right sides facing, and transfer the pattern to it. Mark any openings for reversing indicated on the pattern. Sew carefully and evenly along the marked lines, using a stitch length of 1.5–2mm (⅝–¾in).

CUTTING OUT

Cut out the item with a narrow seam allowance of 3–4mm (⅛in). Where there are openings for reversing, cut a wider seam allowance of about 7–8 mm (⁵⁄₁₆in). Cut a notch in the seam allowance where the seam curves sharply inwards.

REVERSING

A pointed wooden garden cane or stick is useful for reversing. Use mainly the blunt end, except for details such as the bill on a bird where you can use the sharp end to carefully push it out. To avoid the stick poking through the fabric, trim the tip slightly to make it less sharp.

To reverse long, thin shapes, such as legs and arms, push the blunt end of the stick against the foot, see Figure D. Start close to the foot and pull the leg down along the stick, see Figure E. Continue to pull the leg down the stick until the tip/foot emerges from the opening. Pull the foot while drawing back the bottom so that the leg turns right side out, see Figure F.

A   B   C

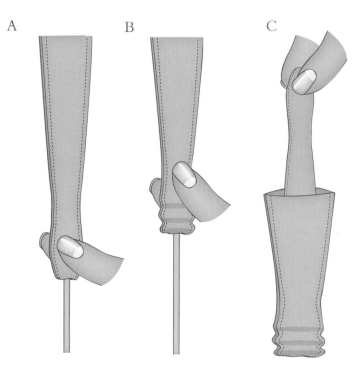

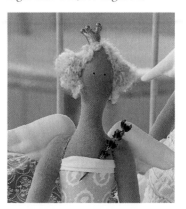

STUFFING

Fold in the extra seam allowance along the opening in the seam. Press the item.

Use your fingers where you can when you are stuffing. Where your fingers won't fit, use the blunt end of a pen or pencil; it will only break through the stuffing and fabric if the tool is too thin.

Push the filling loosely into the item; avoid compressing it into a solid mass before it is in position. Push the filling carefully but firmly into place, adding more filling until you have a firm and well-shaped form. Sew up the opening neatly.

GARDEN HELPERS

YOU WILL NEED
- *Non-elastic skin coloured fabric*
- *Fabric for dress and sun hat*
- *Yarn for the hair*
- *Stuffing*
- *Twigs or root threads and thin wire for the wings*

HOW TO MAKE

BODY

Read the section on 'Stuffed Forms' on pages 8–9 before starting.

Cut out the parts for body and arms from the pattern. Put the pieces right sides together and sew around. Leave an opening for the arms and a reversing opening, see Figure A.

Turn the arms right side out and stuff them before you put them inside the body parts. Sew up the opening for the arms so the arms get attached, see Figure B. Make the dress and the sun hat as shown on pages 12–13.

A

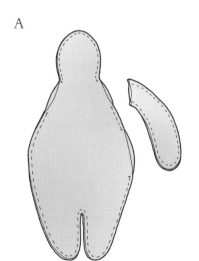

B

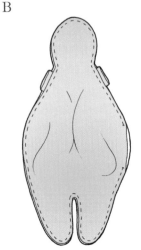

Attach a stick to the back of your angels and insert them into a garden pot filled with oasis.

DRESS

In addition to the fabric you will need iron-on interfacing. Cut out the parts for the dress and the pocket from the pattern. Iron the seam allowance along the edges of the pocket, and sew it on to the right side of one of the dress parts, as marked on the pattern, see Figure C. Put the two parts for the dress right sides together and sew around, see Figure D. Cut out some thin strips of interfacing and tear off the paper. Fold in the seam allowance at the bottom of the dress, on the arms and around the neck. Put the interfacing into the folds and iron, see Figure E. Turn the dress right side out and iron again.

C

D

E

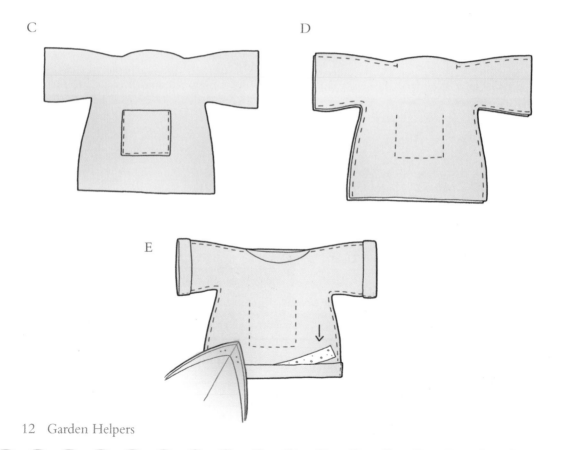

SUN HAT

Dress the figure before you glue or sew on the hair and hat. Cut out the parts for the hat using the pattern. Put the parts right sides together and sew around, see Figure F. Turn the hat right side out and iron. Push the piece with the reversing opening into the other part, see Figure G. Fold out the brim and iron, see Figure H.

WINGS

Make a bundle of twigs or root threads and tie it together with some wire. Tack (baste) it on to the back of the angel.

Use small twigs to create a cute little wreath for your garden helper to hold.

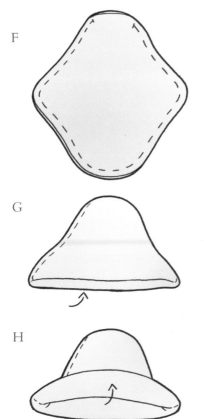

F

G

H

ALL DRESSED UP

YOU WILL NEED

- *Flesh-coloured fabric*
- *Material for dress, pantaloons and wings*
- *Thin fibre felt (optional)*
- *Stuffing*
- *Ribbon and jewels for necklace*
- *Paint for shoes*
- *Halo*
- *Figure stand (optional)*

HOW TO MAKE

BODY

Read the section on 'Stuffed Forms' on pages 8–9 before starting.

Sew together a strip of flesh-coloured fabric and a strip of dress material for the body. Iron apart the seam allowances and fold the assembled strip of material right side to right side.

Draw the outline of the body so that the join between flesh fabric and dress material is roughly as indicated by the dotted line in the pattern. Sew together and fold the flesh-coloured fabric and the material for the arms in the same way as for the body; then draw the arms.

The beautiful angels shown here are about 48cm (19in) tall.

Fold the material for the legs double and draw the legs. Sew around the parts, see Figure A.

Cut out, turn inside out, iron and stuff the body and arms as described on pages 8–9.

If you want to be able to bend the legs of the figure, first stuff half the leg, then sew a seam across before stuffing the rest, see Figure B.

PANTALOONS

The pantaloons are simply made by attaching two trouser legs to the body when attaching the legs. Fold material for the trouser legs right side to right side and draw the outline. Sew around and cut out. Fold up the seam allowance at the bottom and fix with a few stitches or some fabric adhesive before turning inside out and ironing. Thread the legs into the trouser legs so that the openings are together and sew a seam across the openings to keep everything in place, see Figure C.

Fold in the seam allowance around the opening on the body, insert the legs and sew in place. Fold in the seam allowance round the openings on the arms. Place the shoulders against the openings and attach them by sewing round the openings so that the arms hang straight down beside the body, see Figure D on page 18.

SKIRT

Cut out a piece of dress material measuring 36 × 25cm (14 × 10in) and add a seam allowance. Fold the skirt double right side to right side so that it is 18cm (7in) wide and sew along the open edge.

A

B   C

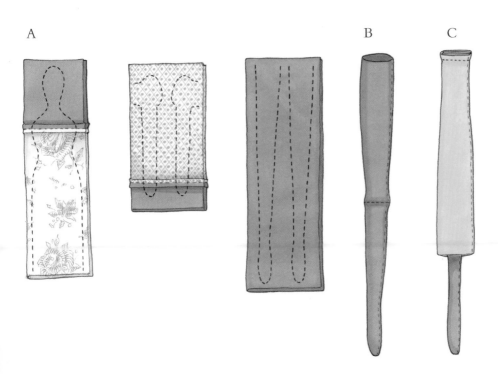

Fold the edge inwards and iron and sew a seam along the bottom edge of the skirt. Fold in the seam allowance at the top and attach the skirt in pleats around the angel, with the seam in the skirt at the back. The skirt should be attached fairly high up on the angel's body, about 2cm (¾in) from the dress edge over the bust.

WINGS

The pattern for the wings has a fold-line on it and should be flipped to make the second wing.

If desired, iron thin fibre felt onto the wrong side of the wing material for a smoother appearance and fold the material right side to right side. Draw the outline of the wings on the material and cut out. Make sure that you cut through the seam allowance where the seam is turned inwards and turn the wings fully inside out with the help of a wooden stick.

Iron the wings and sew seams using a sewing machine a short distance up from the wing tips as indicated in the pattern, see Figure E.

Stuff the channels created between the seams using a wooden stick and stuff the rest of the wings firmly before sewing up the reversing opening. Stitch the wings to the figure, using embroidery yarn and a bodkin.

D

FINISHING TOUCHES

If desired, attach a narrow ribbon and a jewel to make a necklace around the angel's neck.

Make hair and face as described on page 8. Use a ready-made halo or make one out of zinc wire or similar and push it well into the head.

Paint the shoes with a water-based craft paint or textile paint. Mark the area to be painted with an invisible ink pen or a thin ball-point pen and paint with a small, flat brush. The angels have small shoes, painted as indicated by the lowest dotted line shown on the pattern.

Attach the angel to a doll stand by sharpening the end of the rod with a pencil sharpener and pushing it up into the angel until the feet are on the base of the stand. If the angel is to be hung up to display, sew a small ribbon loop to the top of the back.

E

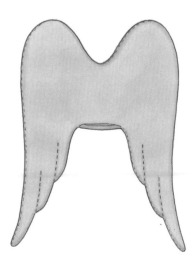

ANGEL APPLIQUÉ

YOU WILL NEED
- *Flesh-coloured fabric*
- *Material for dress and wings*
- *Brown craft paint or textile paint*
- *Sand-coloured or brown stamp pad ink (optional)*
- *A little stuffing*
- *Embroidery thread*
- *Cord and jewels for decoration*
- *Jewellery adhesive*

HOW TO MAKE
Fold material for the wings, body and dress right side to right side. Trace the parts and sew around the edges, see Figure A. Cut out the parts and cut slits into the seam allowance where the edge curves inwards; turn the parts inside out and iron. The dress is turned inside out through an opening made in one of the layers of material.

Paint the hair, push a little stuffing into the body and tie a cord around the neck for the necklace. Place the wings, bust and dress on the background material and attach using pins. The dress should have a pleat at the top. Tack into place.

Sew decorative seams with brown thread on the wings as shown by the dotted line in the pattern. Sew the plaits on each side of the head using brown embroidery thread. Attach the halo using brown thread. Make a face as described on page 8 and attach jewels using jewellery adhesive for decoration.

A

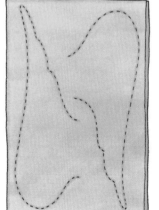
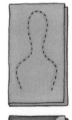

Brush the angel's wings with a small brown or red ink pad to create a shadow effect.

TWO FRIENDS

YOU WILL NEED

- *Fabric for the body, arms and legs*
- *Patterned fabric for the corset (optional)*
- *Fabric offcuts and remnants of old clothes/furnishings for the underwear*
- *Fabric for the wings*
- *Lace, ribbon and buttons for decorating*
- *Stuffing*
- *Doll's hair*
- *Paint for the eyes; blusher or lipstick for the cheeks*
- *Mini gold crowns*
- *Lavender sprigs (optional)*
- *Doll stand (optional)*

HOW TO MAKE

There are two variations on the pattern for the angel, one for the small angel and the other for the long angel, but only one method of making the body.

BODY

Read the section on 'Stuffed Forms' on pages 8–9 before starting.

Sew together a strip of fabric for the head and chest and a strip of patterned fabric for the corset (if using). Press the seam allowances against each other. Fold the piece of fabric double, right sides facing.

These lovable ladies offer you the chance to get creative with remnants of old fabrics.

Transfer the body pattern to it and sew around the outline, see Figure A. Fold the fabric for the arms and legs double, transfer the pattern pieces and sew around all of them, see Figure B.

Cut out all the pieces, turn them right side out and press. Press in the extra seam allowance along the openings on the body and arms before you stuff them.

For the long angel, stuff the legs up to the dotted line on the pattern and sew right across before stuffing the rest of the legs, see Figure C, so that you can bend them.

Stuff the whole leg of the small angel. Pin the legs for the small angel in the opening on the body and stitch the legs in place, see Figure D. Sew a folded strip of fabric, or a length of lace or ribbon, to the top edge of the corset before you attach the arms, see Figure D. Attach the arms later if the angel is going to be dressed in the sleeve dress (see opposite).

A

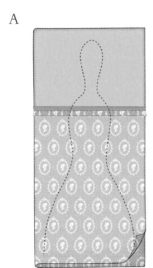

B

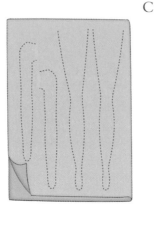

C

D

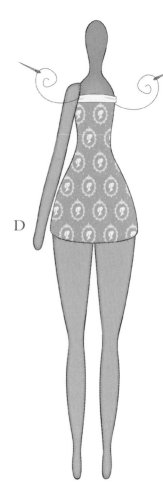

PANTALOONS

Fold the fabric for the pantaloons double and cut out the pattern, placed on the fold. Sew the two pieces together, right sides facing, see Figure E. Fold up the seam allowance on each leg and stitch. Sew on a strip of lace or ribbon if desired, see Figure F. Fold the pantaloons so that the seams are aligning and sew the legs, see Figure G. Turn the pantaloons right side out and press. Dress the figure and fold in the waist if it is too high and will show over the skirt edge. Stitch in place.

SLEEVE DRESS

The short angel's dress is made from a cut-off blouse sleeve. Turn the sleeve inside out and sew a seam on each side to make it fit the angel. Hem the edge of the dress. The button on the sleeve is on the back of the angel. Put the dress on the angel before you attach her arms so that you can pull the dress over the chest properly.

E 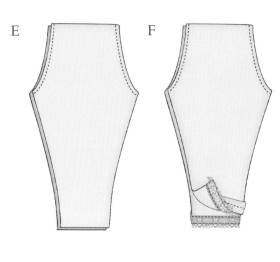 F

G

SKIRT

For the long angel the skirt has two layers, but you can use only one if you want to. The fabric should be 70cm (27½in) wide to make it flouncy. The bottom skirt is 20cm (8in) long and the top layer 18cm (7in) long, plus seam allowances. Fold in the seam allowance along the bottom edge and stitch in place. If you want to decorate with lace or ribbon, sew them on before you fold the skirt double and sew it together.

Fold in the top edge and sew with long machine stitches without fastening the thread ends, see Figure H. Then carefully pull the thread on the reverse side to gather the strip until the desired length, see Figure I. Put the skirt on the figure and stitch low down on the waist. The top skirt is sewn with a row of long machine stitches and gathered about 7cm (2¾in) from the bottom edge as a nice detail.

For the short angel, the bottom skirt is 14cm (5½in) wide and the top 12cm (4¾in). The lengths are the same as for the long angel.

H

I

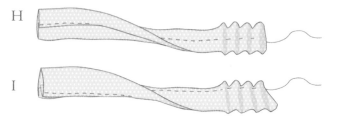

WINGS, HAIR AND FACE

Fold the fabric for the wings double, transfer the pattern, flipping it to make the second wing, and sew around the outlines. Cut out, snipping into the seam allowance where the seam points sharply inwards. Use a wooden stick to turn the wings right side out. Press the wings and top stitch from the edge of the wings inwards, see Figure J.

Stuff the channels between the top stitching with the help of the stick, then stuff the rest of the wings before you sew up the opening. Tack the wings on to the back of the angel.

Attach the hair and add the face, as instructed on page 8. Attach the crown. Decorate the skirt with buttons and add a lavender sprig to the corset if desired.

J

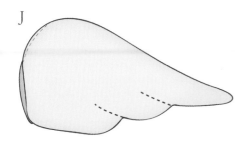

BY THE SEA

YOU WILL NEED

- *Materials for the long or short angel, with corset in swimsuit fabric*
- *Additional swimsuit fabric for the pantaloons, skirt and collar*
- *Stuffing*
- *White velvet ribbon, 3mm (⅛in) wide*
- *Three white pearls, 3mm (⅛in) in diameter*
- *Shell buttons*
- *Fine wire (optional)*

HOW TO MAKE

BODY

Read the section on 'Stuffed Forms' on pages 8–9 before starting.

Make either the long or short angel following the instructions on pages 22 and 24, using swimsuit fabric for the 'corset'.

These bold costumes are similar to the first swimsuits from the mid 19th century.

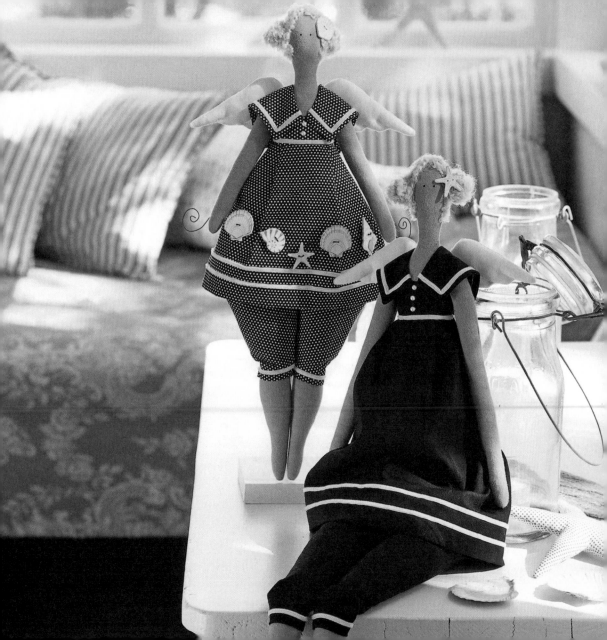

PANTALOONS

Make up the pantaloons in the swimsuit fabric as instructed on page 25. Stitch white velvet ribbon 6–7mm (¼in) from the leg bottoms.

SWIMSUIT SKIRT

Cut a piece of fabric for the swimsuit skirt 42 × 22cm (16½ × 9in) for the long angel and 42 × 14cm (16½ × 5½in) for the short angel, plus seam allowances. Fold in, press and hem one of the long sides. Stitch one length of ribbon about 1.5cm (⅝in) from the edge, then another about 1cm (⅜in) in from the first. Fold the skirt double, right sides facing. Sew up the open side. Fold in the seam allowance around the top of the skirt and gather (see page 26), then stitch the skirt to the angel high up on the waist (see photo). Stitch ribbon around the waist just above the top edge of the skirt.

FINISHING TOUCHES

Fold the fabric for the collar double, right sides facing. Transfer the pattern, sew around the outline and cut out. Turn right side out and press. Sew ribbon around the collar 5mm (³⁄₁₆in) from the outside edge, see Figure A. Attach to the bodice front and back with a few stitches, see Figure B. Sew pearls to the front.

Complete the wings, hair and face (see page 27). Stitch a shell button to the hair. You can also thread more shell buttons on to wire, curl the wire ends and attach to the angel's hands.

A

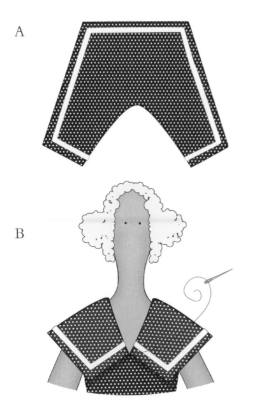

B

BED TIME

HOW TO MAKE

BODY

Read the section on 'Stuffed Forms' on pages 8–9 before starting.

Fold the fabric over double and trace the body, arms and legs. Sew around the edges, see Figure A. Cut out the pieces, remembering to add an extra seam allowance for the openings. Turn right sides out, iron and stuff as described on pages 8–9. Only the lower part of the arms should be padded to make the arms hang nicely.

Insert the seam allowance at the top of the legs into the opening at the bottom of the body, and sew the opening closed, fastening the legs as you go. Fold in the seam allowance at the top of the arms and stitch to the body, see Figure B.

A

B

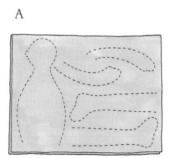

This sleepy angel would make a perfect gift or bedroom accessory.

NIGHTSHIRT

Cut out the two identical nightshirt pieces and two sleeves, following the pattern. Add extra seam allowance at the bottom of the nightshirt and ends of the sleeves. Sew together across the shoulders, open out and sew in the sleeves.

Fold the nightshirt, right sides together, and sew up the sides and along the sleeves, see Figure C. Fold up the hem at the bottom of the nightshirt and sleeves. Cut strips of iron-on tape and place them inside the hems and iron to fasten.

Fold the collar fabric in half and trace the collar. Sew around it, see Figure D. Cut it out, turn right side out and iron the collar.

Turn the nightshirt right sides out and tuck in the seam allowance around the neckline. Fit the collar into the neckline and stitch, see Figure E. Fold the collar down, and iron. Put the nightshirt on the stuffed figure.

WINGS

Fold the fabric in half, right sides together, and place two layers of wadding underneath. Trace the wing pattern and sew around, see Figure F. Cut out the wings, and cut notches in the seam allowance where the seams swing inwards. Cut an opening through one layer of the fabric, as shown on the pattern. Turn right sides out, and iron the wings. If you wish, you can add decorative stitches or quilt around the edge of the wings. Stitch the wings on to the figure with the opening facing the back, so that it is hidden.

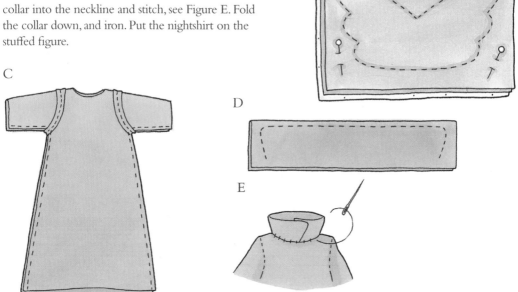

C

D

E

F

NIGHTCAP

To make the nightcap, fold the fabric in half, trace the pattern and add extra seam allowance at the bottom. Sew around it, see Figure G. Cut out and turn right side out. Fold in the seam allowance at the bottom, and iron before putting the hat on the figure. Tack the hat on to the head with a few stitches at the back and on either side.

Put the dress on the figure, and fasten it with stitched on buttons. Attach the wings. Make the hair as described on page 8 and tack on the hat with a few stitches on either side. Add a face for the angel as described on page 8.

PILLOW

Fold the fabric for the pillow in half, right sides together. Trace the pattern and sew around it. Cut it out and cut an opening through one layer of fabric where marked on the pattern. Turn the right way out, iron and fill the pillow with stuffing. Stitch the pillow on to the figure and the hand to the pillow, so that the angel appears to be holding it. Fasten the other hand to the face if desired.

G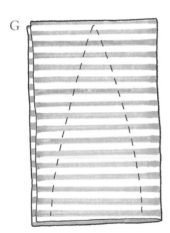

Use striped fabrics for a great bed time look. You could even match the nightshirt with your own.

HOME SWEET HOME

HOW TO MAKE

BODY

Read the section on 'Stuffed Forms' on pages 8–9 before starting.

Fold the skin fabric double and trace the body, arms and legs from the pattern; then sew around the parts. Cut out the parts, turn them inside out and iron them. Stuff the legs up to the dotted line on the pattern and sew a seam straight across before stuffing the rest of the leg, see Figure A. Stuff the body, fold in the seam allowance around the opening and insert the legs. Only the lower part of the arms should be stuffed, so that the arms hang nicely when the angel has been dressed up, and so that they can be bent and fixed at the desired angles. Tack on the legs and arms, see Figure B.

A   B

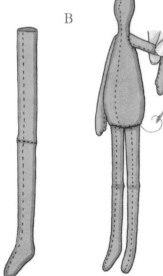

36

The felt material used for this angel gives the effect of a warm fleece.

PANTALOONS

Cut out the parts of the pantaloons as in the pattern, adding a seam allowance at the waist and at the bottom of the legs. Note that the parts should be double, so that the fold is in the centre of each of the two pieces. Place the two parts right side to right side and sew them together, see Figure C. Fold the pantaloons so that the seams are on top of each other and sew the legs, see Figure D.

Fold open the seam allowance at the bottom of the pants, remove small pieces of glue from the backing paper of Bondaweb and push them into the fold on either side. Iron the fold so that it sticks.

Turn the pantaloons inside out, put them on the figure and tack them round the waist.

SKIRT

Cut some material measuring about 40 × 25cm (15½ × 10in), fold it double, right side to right side, and sew the edges together on the open side. Sew the seam allowance around the edge. Put the skirt on the angel, fold pleats at the waist and fix with pins before tacking the skirt in place.

C   D

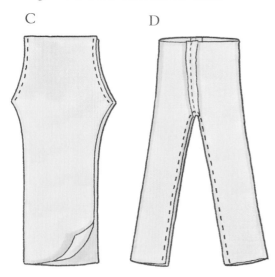

SWEATER

The pattern for the sweater is marked with a fold line and should be cut double. Woollen felt doesn't fray, so seam allowances at openings aren't necessary at the places marked with dotted lines on the pattern.

Place two pieces of felt, large enough for the sweater, right side to right side and trace the pattern. Sew around the outline of the sweater, see Figure E. Cut out the sweater and turn it inside out. Put the sweater on the angel, see Figure F, then fold the collar of the sweater double inwards towards the angel's neck, see Figure G. Then fold half the double collar out again, see Figure H.

E

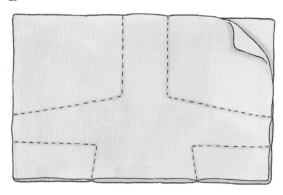

F

G

H

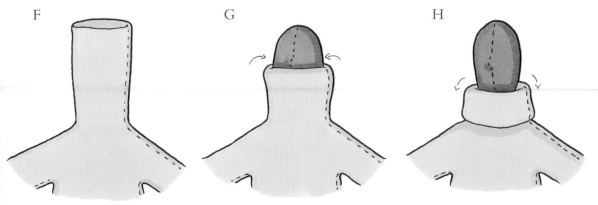

I

SLIPPERS

Fold material for the slippers right side to right side. Trace the shape, sew and cut the curve at the opening of the slipper, see Figure I, then turn the slipper so that the right side is out. Fold the part double so that the fold is in the middle, as shown with a dotted line on the pattern. Trace half the slipper and sew round, see Figure J, then cut out the slipper and press the toe flat using an iron. Trace the small curve in the pattern so that the toe of the slipper is rounded and sew it, see Figure K, before cutting the toe on the outside of the seam. Turn the slipper inside out so that the seam is inside.

J

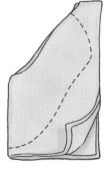

K

WINGS

Cut out a piece of material twice as large as the wings and a piece of cotton padding the size of the wings. Fold the material double right side to right side and place the cotton padding underneath. Trace the pattern on the material and sew around the edge, see Figure L. Cut out the wings and turn them inside out before sewing up the reversing opening.

Tack or glue the wings to the angel and attach the slippers with a couple of stitches at the back.

HAIR AND FACE

Make a face for your angel as described on page 8.

To create a fancy hairstyle, stick three long pieces of steel wire through the angel's head so that you have six steel wires coming out. You can use a large bodkin to pull the wire through, but if this proves to be too difficult, stick six lengths of steel wire into the head.

Tie a long piece of doll's hair around one of the six wires and twist it back and forth on the back and top of the angel's head, eventually winding the hair around the wire ends too, see Figure M. When you have covered the whole of the angel's head with doll's hair and wrapped hair some distance along each of the steel wires, bend the remaining uncovered wire in and twist it around itself close to the angel's head.

Finally, tack along the middle of the head with a few stitches to keep the hair in place, see Figure N.

You can give your angels hairstyles with only two plaits by following the same procedure but by using just one or two lengths of wire instead of six.

L

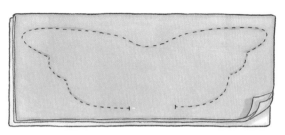

M

N

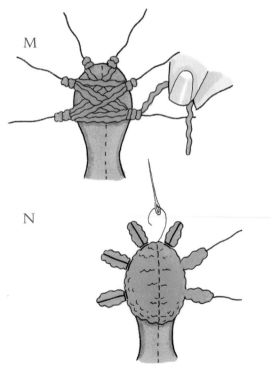

CORNETS

YOU WILL NEED

- *Skin-coloured, light and dark brown linen for faces*
- *Various fabrics for the wings*
- *Various fabrics and linings for the cornets*
- *Wadding*
- *Stuffing*
- *Toy hair, blond, light and dark brown*
- *Twigs, beads and thin steel wire for the wreath*
- *Cord for hanging*
- *Embroidery threads and fabric paints for the face*

HOW TO MAKE

CORNET

Note that the cornet pattern must be placed on the folded edge of the fabric which is double with right sides together. When opened out the fold is in the middle, see Figure A.

Cut out one cornet in fabric, one in lining and two in wadding. The fabric and lining are placed on top of each other, right sides together. One piece of the wadding is placed underneath, the other on the top. Sew the parts together along the curved edge on the top of the cornet, see Figure B.

A

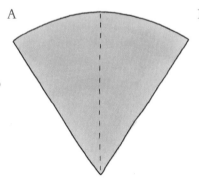

B

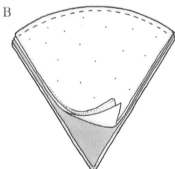

These cornet angels are sure to appeal when filled to the brim with sweet treats.

Unfold the cornet, so that the seam is across the middle, and fold it right sides together the opposite way. Sew leaving an opening in the lining, see Figure C. Trim any excessive seam allowances and turn the cornet right sides out. Sew the opening closed, and push the lining well into the fabric part, using a plant stick. Iron the cornet.

C

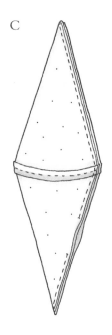

FACE AND WINGS

Fold the fabric for the head in half, right sides together, and trace the head pattern. Sew around it, cut out, turn the right way out, iron, fill with stuffing and stitch the opening, following the instructions on page 9, see Figure D. Make the face and attach the hair, see page 8.

Make the wings as described on page 34. Tack them on to the cornet, so that the middle of the wings protrudes approximately 1cm (½in) above the edge of the cornet, see Figure E. Stitch the head firmly on to both the cornet and the wings.

Use pins to fasten the cord on either side of the cornet. Adjust so that it hangs fairly straight. If the angel tips too far forwards or backwards, the cord must be adjusted accordingly, before it is stitched on.

D

E

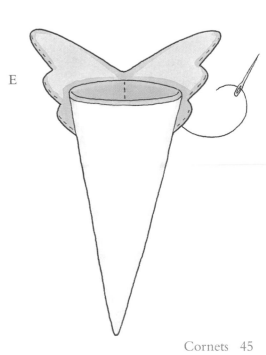

Cornets 45

SUPPLIERS

UK

Panduro Hobby
Westway House
Transport Avenue
Brentford
Middlesex
TW8 9HF
Tel: 020 8566 1680
trade@panduro.co.uk
www.pandurohobby.co.uk

Coast and Country
Crafts & Quilts
8 Sampson Gardens
Ponsanooth, Truro
Cornwall
TR3 7RS
Tel: 01872 863894
www.coastandcountrycrafts.co.uk

Fred Aldous Ltd.
37 Lever Street
Manchester
M1 1LW
Tel: 08707 517301
www.fredaldous.co.uk

The Sewing Bee
52 Hillfoot Street
Dunoon, Argyll
PA23 7DT
Tel: 01369 706879
www.thesewingbee.co.uk

Puddlecrafts
7 St. Clair Park
Route Militaire
St. Sampson
Guernsey
GY2 4DX
Tel: 01481 245441
www.puddlecrafts.co.uk

The Fat Quarters
5 Choprell Road
Blackhall Mill
Newcastle
NE17 7TN
Tel: 01207 565728
www.thefatquarters.co.uk

Threads and Patches
48 Aylesbury Street
Fenny Stratford
Bletchley
Milton Keynes
MK2 2BU
Tel: 01908 649687
www.threadsandpatches.co.uk

USA

Coats and Clark USA
PO Box 12229
Greenville
SC29612-0229
Tel: 0800 648 1479
www.coatsandclark.com

Connecting Threads
13118 NE 4th Street
Vancouver
WA 9884
www.connectingthreads.com

eQuilter.com
5455 Spine Road, Suite E
Boulder
CO 80301
www.equilter.com

Hamels Fabrics
5843 Lickman Road
Chilliwack
British Columbia
V2R 4B5
www.hamelsfabrics.com

Keepsake Quilting
Box 1618 Center Harbor
NH 03226
www.keepsakequilting.com

The Craft Connection
21055 Front Street
PO Box 1088
Onley
VA 23418
www.craftconn.com

INDEX

TEMPLATES

All templates need to be enlarged by 400%.
Add seam allowance for all templates, except
for the appliqué shapes.

Garden Helpers
(page 10)

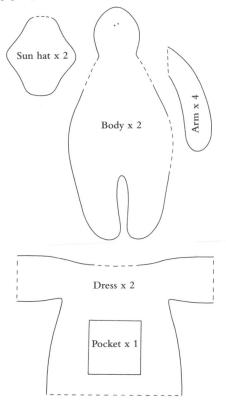

Sun hat x 2

Body x 2

Arm x 4

Dress x 2

Pocket x 1

Cornets
(page 42)

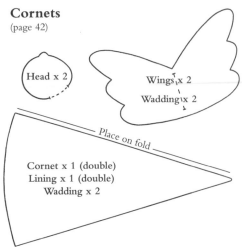

Head x 2

Wings x 2

Wadding x 2

Place on fold

Cornet x 1 (double)
Lining x 1 (double)
Wadding x 2

All Dressed Up
(page 14)

Angel Appliqué
(page 20)

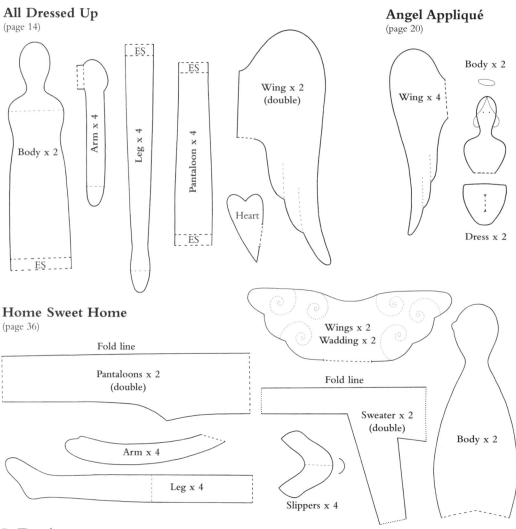

Body x 2

Arm x 4

Leg x 4

ES

ES

Pantaloon x 4

ES

ES

Wing x 2
(double)

Heart

Wing x 4

Body x 2

Dress x 2

Home Sweet Home
(page 36)

Fold line

Pantaloons x 2
(double)

Wings x 2
Wadding x 2

Fold line

Sweater x 2
(double)

Body x 2

Arm x 4

Leg x 4

Slippers x 4

48   Templates

Two Friends and By the Sea

(page 22)   (page 28)

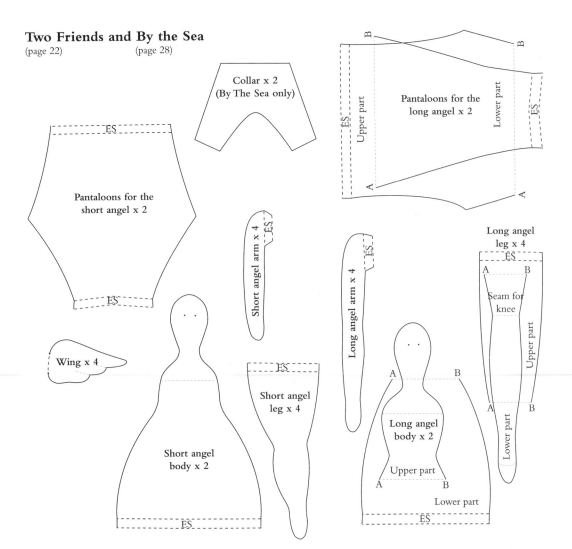

Collar x 2
(By The Sea only)

Pantaloons for the
long angel x 2

ES

Upper part

Lower part

ES

B

B

A

A

ES

Pantaloons for the
short angel x 2

ES

Short angel arm x 4

ES

Long angel arm x 4

ES

Long angel
leg x 4

ES

A   B

Seam for
knee

Upper part

A   B

Lower part

Upper part

Wing x 4

Short angel
leg x 4

ES

A   B

Long angel
body x 2

Upper part

A   B

Lower part

Short angel
body x 2

ES

ES

Bed Time
(page 32)

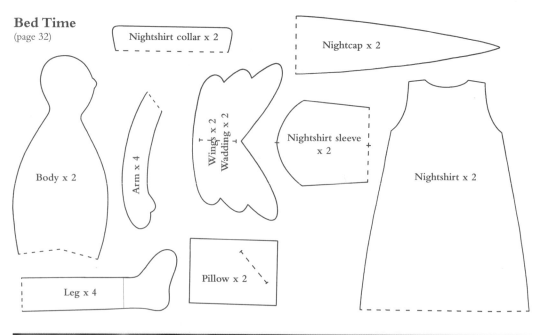

Nightshirt collar x 2

Nightcap x 2

Body x 2

Arm x 4

Wings x 2
Wadding x 2

Nightshirt sleeve x 2

Nightshirt x 2

Leg x 4

Pillow x 2

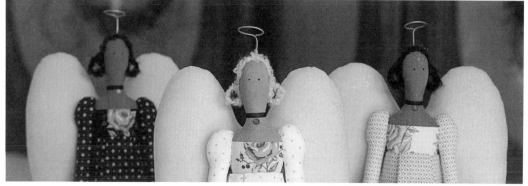